SLOW RUNNER

poems by

Marjorie Deiter Keyishian

Finishing Line Press
Georgetown, Kentucky

SLOW RUNNER

Copyright © 2007 by Marjorie Deiter Keyishian

ISBN 978-1-59924-164-7 First Edition

All rights reserved under International and Pan-American Copyright Conventions. No part of this book may be reproduced in any manner whatsoever without written permission from the publisher, except in the case of brief quotations embodied in critical articles and reviews.

ACKNOWLEDGMENTS

Grateful acknowledgment is made to the editors and publishers of the following journals in which these poems first appeared:

"Slow Runner," *Massachusetts Review*; "Time," "The Real Island," "Time," *Ararat*; "Craft," *Works*; "Places," *Black Mountain II Review*; "Gift," "Among Dervishes," *The English Record*; "Alchemy," *The Literary Review*; "Fear," *Phoebe*; "Prayer," *Footwork*; "Sunflowers," *Snowy Egret*; "Shoes," *Journal of New Jersey Poets*

Editor: **Leah Maines**
Cover Art: **Oriole Feshbach**
Inside Art: **Emily Keyishian**
Author Photo: *Morristown Daily Record*. Used with permission.

Printed in the USA on acid-free paper.

Order online: www.finishinglinepress.com
also available on www.amazon.com

Author inquiries and mail orders:
Finishing Line Press
P. O. Box 1626
Georgetown, Kentucky 40324
U. S. A.

CONTENTS

Slow Runner ~page~ 3
Time ~page~ 4
The Home ~page~ 5
Sunflowers ~page~ 6
Fall ~page~ 7
Cardinal ~page~ 8
Craft ~page~ 9
Places ~page~ 10
Among Dervishes ~page~ 11
Alchemy ~page~ 12
Bird and Beast ~page~ 13
Prayer ~page~ 14
In Space ~page~ 15
Fear ~page~ 16
Aphrodite and the Iconoclasts ~page~ 17
Sidewalk Artists ~page~ 18
Gift ~page~ 20
The Venturer ~page~ 21
Crystal Palace ~page~ 22
The Real Island ~page~ 23
Shoes ~page~ 24
About the Author ~page~ 29

To my family, all of you, and of course Harry

"At evening, casual flocks of pigeons make
Ambiguous undulations as they sink,
Downward to darkness, on extended wings."

—Wallace Stevens

SLOW RUNNER

Remember when death was brand new,
a chick hatching wet and unlovely,
waving tiny delicate wings to dry off its feathers?

Remember when death came for one's grandma,
the absolutely beloved, smelly little woman,
whose nourishing was round, that early queen,
the shape of what really was, alchemist
of squash and corpses of chickens?

Later, we hardly noticed how it plucked
up old men and old women, blurs at the edges
of photos whose absence was less weighty than passing seasons,
and cousins one had heard about but barely remembered.

Now he stands at the bottom of your bed, my dear,
Sticks to you as if you were tar paper
and he, so grey so small, grows somewhat larger
every single day, whether or not we pay attention.

And the conversation dribbles into coughs, shrugs.
Both you and he look out past smoky streaks at the uniform
grey of a February sky. Someone could find shape,
a pattern of dark and light, delicate as fingerprints
no one particularly wants to read. Mr. Clean wipes them down.

Both you and he have nothing much to say.
You rage from time to time.
He swallows and hiccups.
Or vice versa.

TIME

Of course, music will do it or the taste
of a cake. The smell of dust in a shuttered
room wakes Time. He stretches, winks, and lays waste
the careful walls, knocks to bits bricks mortared
with safe intervals. All the sheltered years
are melting. A door to the woods opens.
Cool and rich is the green light back where
the scruff and mess of growing things blends
uneasily all the naked hours, moist
as leeches, waiting, waiting, patiently.
Anything can wake them. Bloodhungry, they eat
all we've laid by to sate them. He's loose. See
Time reduce us to roots, to loss, to mud.
He's in us, of us, circling with our blood.

THE HOME

At first, the hulks, the battered wrecks,
washed up on this linoleum beach,
subvert all we know of self and soul. Lost,
they wander the polished halls, tended by
paid strangers who often are gentle, round
them up, lead them home to the neat, white
beds. Their names blazoned on numbered doors,
their bleeding wounds tended, their soiled
clothes laundered and folded into drawers,

they must be told that no bus stops at the door
to take them home, that the fare has been paid,
that they may, unashamed, rest here, who have
wheeled themselves up and down, up and down,
the storied building of their lives, fearful
that somehow they have fallen out of favor,
and that is why they can no longer walk without
cages nor dance, as if they'd failed somewhere
to do what was right and this ruin, the claws,
the curved backs were their just reward.

They must be told over and again that now
this is home and that they are truly whole
and that we who come, day after shattering day,
know they are truly who they say they are,
they who taught us love and teach us still.

SUNFLOWERS

These sunflowers are heavy islands. Those
slender stems that root them to earth bend,
graceful as any wild horse, sun dappling
their green and shining necks—islands
visited by small birds and bees resting
or harvesting sweet nectar, seeds, aphids—
islands tall as young ailanthus trees. I,
taller than all, am Jack's lonely giant,
hungry for blood and lost, wanting
the long and heavy fall, perched, as a bird
on a branch, on the walls of this high
stone house, waiting to fly, to fall through green,
to join, light as a striped and hungry bee,
the golden, the vibrant green, the sunflower.

FALL

Under a hot sun, I'm caught in the woods,
calling for a child that entered and has
not been seen for some time. When the wind
blows, I hear her. Where in the round of trees?
If the wind shakes trees till they're naked,
will she be there, or will the leaves, piled high
and higher, the crisp leaves, hide her, deep
                    in woods?

CARDINAL

In the clutter of the ordinary,
a red shirt tail hangs out;
the pertinent cardinal measures
brown fields and sky. Does he decide
to land on a branch? shaking
loose the ragged leaf that scraped
across the smoky glass of a kitchen
window, that sorry remnant of green,
finger tapping in unhallowed night
where the dead walk and chat,
as if waking us were not important
as if nothing in space minded that
we quaked through the little dark time
and slept finally when light quickened,

waking late to the irreverent bird,
bold and erratic,
hanging like a mulberry on brown
unworthy boughs.

CRAFT

All winter, I worked with iridescent
feathers, fashioning flies rich as purple.
Of reds and blues, I wove intimate crescents;
intricate skips and stops of their supple
dance, I foresaw; wonderful as dragon
flies, the skitter, the flick, of eye and wrist
stippling a tense surface of still and sun
checkered water. The trout that snap and twist
are cunning, ribald and cold to my lure.
Their shadows laugh on a surface dappled
with insects and clusters of eggs. Secure
in raucous plenty, trout glide; they grapple.
Intense and glittering, beyond any fly
I tied by firelight, is the fish's eye.

PLACES

This hush in the woods has a name: Stephen,
St. David, or Apollo's Grove. That bird's
voice isn't accidental: Pan's piping,
plucking strings he planted at the lusty
leap of generation, long years ago.
Beginnings are like that.

      Waiting millennia for worshippers,
shaping forests as spiders spin their webs,
he's caught whole tribes, for a time, with one tree,
with a whisper of clear water, with moss
on a rock ringed round by trees. Listen.
His voice. He's quarreling with the sea gull.

AMONG DERVISHES

Across the flat plains of Kansas
and Oklahoma, the untidy
cyclone wheels round, an unruly
intrusion, drawing dust that blurs
and confuses the bold circle
of sky, stretching equidistant
from a center made by a still man.

Over a flat sea, waterspouts
walk, bowing like mating birds,
formal as birds caught in a dance
of generation.
      Whirling and
still in deserts are dervishes,
static and turning in their
absolute lust after motion.
Sentient as the waterspout
are their holy actions that
flatten what rises above the sand.

ALCHEMY

Carpenters are in love with wood;
A hand on the bole of the living tree
tells them the number of running board feet.
Gnarls of hard winter, limbs lost to ice, might
save a tree, after all, for a season.
Carpenters are in love with the rasp, file,
the teeth of saws, the beat of hammers:
what transforms the exuberance of green
into something other (what's smooth under hand).

Bakers take fine flour (berries of wheat, rye,
threshed and ground by stone or steel rollers)
and yeast (that smells of loamy fields and grows,
there, in the kitchen, warmed with milk, water)
honey, knead alive the ball of dough; smell
the loaf baking in the killing oven;
break hot the new bread; dip it in butter,
salt it, and eat the whole—in the new house
that smells so sweetly of sawdust and loaves.

Time's fine chisel etches lines on faces,
molds the whole over into something else.
New shapes emerge from ball of baby, stretch,
smile, and, stoopshouldered, sink to sagging egg
of age perched uneasily on an earth
which waits for that further transformation.
Metamorphosis is what we know of time.
We are alchemists—loving change, not gold.

BIRD AND BEAST

Black crow flapping heavy wings lands.
The branch, high as a second story,
shakes and shakes. The fragile tracery
of branches barely supports his weight.
Nothing's light about crows;
their flight is all effort.

Squirrel up from the ground arcs
from tree to tree, flies, topping trees,
tipping new green. The thinnest twigs,
farthest extension in high blue
day, scarcely shake as he passes;
he's gone as he touches.

And the crow hangs on and on.
Black caw and clumsy wings
beat air and leaf. Each
step of his passing goes
slowly, underlined by his effort,
attended by noise.

PRAYER

Those great wheels of talking stars are old news.
All that radiance, wispy spokes and all
fertile journeys, happened so far ago

that we here are echoes. What else is earth
but echo of some exuberance? Atom
wrenched out of shape, of place, sent to spin
into a sun we never stop worshipping.

How would we dare to sleep without whisper:
a prayer that morning is possible? Love,
this hot artifact, warms into being,

here—so far beneath that glitter we thought
cold—is prayer. If no star breaks apart
in the night, a scrawl of color, that streak
of purple hot in the sky, answers us.

If no filament screams our way this night
(to undo us), day will happen once more.

It's better, my love, to urge our star on
its hard way, through this crowded galaxy
than to lie apart, as once we thought stars did.

IN SPACE

When a star's cycle makes no sense,
a dark sister is presumed: two stars
intertwine, gesture by dipping
in passing, in a regular roll.

Earth wobbles in turning to accommodate
a moon that trails it through space.
Both earth and moon are invisible.
But watching the sun would tell it,
rock and roll of its trail picking out
each of its planets, even the moon.

I have heard that oceans salute her,
the moon, that waves lift to her turning,
disappointed drops falling farther and farther
behind as she passes, and the blood
of women joins in such cycles.

Sarah, standing as soon as she was able,
reached out. Surely, the yellow circle
was a ball I could catch for her,
leave in her crib. Is it necessary
to say I could not? That we
bend to her turning and she to ours?

I, too, wobble from straight line or cycle,
pulls of each of you there in my movements,
a cord radiating, beaten gold stretching.
To you, dear love, I curtsey in passing,
heart rounding outward to touch you in space.

FEAR

He's changing shape again, leaping from corner
to corner, the color of certain times of night,
the white times before the sun decides to rise,
the hot red of exhausted afternoons.
Holding the heart of our world between us,
warm as her chortle, shaky as faces
in a moving mirror, as safe as common
water and often, I remember him,
am the rabbit in the huge, flat field, all
bolt holes closed, and the shadow in the cloud
less sky closing in, the obscene shadow.
A conspiracy of mother gentle
mornings, of afternoons soft as blowing
curtains, and behind them, he is smiling.

APHRODITE AND THE ICONOCLASTS

We're knee deep in shards and dust,
stuck with a puzzle. Someone had caught love,
controlled the stone till it was she. Perhaps
her lost arms would have told us what love is.
Their shattered fragments lie all about.

The raging, upright men whose hammers
broke her spell have melted, too. Long ago,
those lovers of The Word wasted away.
Then stone and their dry bones were joined . Now
wind catches them. The righteous men can dance
with stone. They are the motes in our hungry eyes.

SIDEWALK ARTIST

Slim and dapper as a snake charmer,
he catches wayfarers, pulls in strangers
with a smile, with a touch on a sleeve.
He weaves a circle round the slouched hat
left in the gutter, ready for pennies.

He's the sparrow finding crumbs on sidewalks
and rainbows in oily puddles crowded
buses leave behind. City bird, he has
the third eye (the eye that spots cops
and hungry cats) and powerful chalk.

Fingers slicker than a dip's pluck the rose
the sun makes of pebbles stuck in cement,
tough enough for piss and spit and shuffling feet,
draw its intricate petals, its neon halos,
and the brassy smile of fabulous towers.

ABOUT HUNGER

About hunger, about desire,
what we whimper for
in the bleak reaches of night.

At dawn, before want begins,
there is thin light belonging to birds
who eat their weight in seed, in berry,
hour after lustful hour.

Tables groan under the weight
of root, leaf, and meat.
Market, stand, and oven are
quite full. And still, we want.

GIFT

Watch hot tongues of fire lick alive dry wood;
paper, twig, and log catch, spark and dance, join,
while my hot and coursing blood is enclosed,
apart, and safe as any miser's coin
locked in vaulted coffers. This silken skin
between lets nothing through. Pierce it, and I
evaporate. Nothing I do can win
warmth for you. Icy and shuddering, you lie
beside me, you who are what fire I've found.
Your sweet flesh is strange as ice. Falling flakes
of snow can ripen to it. I am bound
to hold you close, but never close enough to make
that gift of warmth. Though my molten core
flow, everything is as it was before.

THE VENTURER

She steps down into her element,
lets bubbles fret her toes. And further,
the waves climb her ankles, chasten knees,
chill womb. Dead center, she plunges,

Strikes out, muscles rippling as water does,
shoulders flexing, belonging.

She aims for the white rim, sirens
on the horizon, of island and island.

Water does not forgive,
takes her, without anger,
the way wind yanks the limb
of an oak, twists leaves,
shunts them first east, then west,
to where, to past where, they hold on.
Still green, silver sides up,
they sail skyward and she seaward.

And on shore they wonder at the arm's rhythm,
At how far from shore the swimmer has gone,
and night coming down and with it
the dangerous turn of the tide.

CRYSTAL PALACE

A flake lands on Noah's jacket.
We marvel at the delicate spokes—
crystal upon falling crystal. Flakes billow.
Weighty flakes pack down. And then
we roll them over and over, mold them,
throwing rounded flakes, whisper into thump:
projectile, meteor, cannon-ball.

Next is the shaping into statue.
We incarnate: dress great cold round
in twig, in hat, put mittens on a fist of snow.

We are ridiculous, waving as we walk
out of the woods, wondering all the way home
whether tomorrow we will walk this way,
and, if we do, whether that snow fellow
will still hold—how close—to the shape we gave it.

THE REAL ISLAND

You, my dear, promised to make with your hands
a house like the one we found the day
we took to the sea, land awash, submerging
behind us, our boat picking its way
through random islands. Above birds flew
contending that the land was theirs.

Wilder than the Innisfree I evoke,
though I don't like bees or honey,
a turning tide ate half the land and spat
it up for sun and birds, for our boat.
Tide measured the time we might remain
beyond small affairs Innisfrees annul.

Our children scattered, squabbling,
loud as gulls and as demanding,
asking that the Stonehenge they'd raised
remain, that the ball the tide'd taken
turn back, that lunch be something other
than lobster or peanut butter.

Cold wind, a turning tide loud as a train,
white slabs dry as soon as the sparkling
sea lets them go to the strong sun: are these
enough to justify labor incessant
as the sea—and all to survive
on a rock the sea has raised and defends?

What could the heart's ear hear?
Rich blood pounding along drowns
out much as we lift and push.
Who, arguing with the sea
for a ball thrown into air and caught
by water, can stop to listen?

SHOES

At 16, he took off, rode rails
past rusting cars piled high as
far mountains, past the romance
of the quarry, jumble of stones,
the lilting cranes, straight out
of black and white movies: guys
thumbing across the wide country,
from one trolley-diner to the next,
sleeping in a jail cell one cold,
starry night thanks to a kind sheriff.

In 1932, he offered his brand new wife half
the rumble seat. And big brother Ben
took them to California where Ben lived
his happily ever after. After that, he
and rambling Rose took the kids upstate
and back. He flew up to Alaska, junketed
down to the Caribbean. Twice he went alone
to Europe. When he died, 34 pairs of shoes,
white patent, black, brown, were lined up
on painted wooden steps, as if they waited
their turn to make an entrance; as if
an audience, poised behind the closet wall,
would clap them home, they climbed the door,
shoes everywhere, hardly a hole, trim shoes.

34 pairs: thin skinned dancing shoes, trim
loafers, in shades of brown & white,
laces and laces tucked in, black galoshes,
metal buckles worn silver,
prim under the dust sifting down.

About autos, he cared less, denting bumpers,
smashing into walls, even the Caddy went un-
polished. He totaled cars in three states,
maybe four. They got him where he wanted
to go, and that was that.

Maps were like tight shoes and confusing.
He kept them handy, but taught us
to keep on moving; even when you're heading
in the wrong direction, to keep rolling.

He tip toed, sashayed, waltzed so
far from the lower East side, bouncing back
over and again and no more.

Those shoes should have been worn down,
tongues hanging out, panting,
soles holey, visible signs of the miles
he'd covered, crossing the continent,
east to west, north to south,
winging across the Atlantic,
the Caribbean, wanting everywhere
and the swing back home. For grins, he'd
tunnel under the Hudson or over the Narrows,
outpacing ferries, freighters, tankers,
odd sailing ships, heeling over in the wind
that pushed him, here and there.

Who is to say that, barefoot, he,
who left no instructions, is not now
on that zig-zag run out past the sun
and Jupiter rounding the Plutonic corner
on his way to the Dog Star and beyond?

Not I, his daughter, finding myself
crossing and recrossing the Hudson,
goaded and goading, still the uneasy child,
occasionally offering lifts
to dangerous strangers
in his honor who told it like
it never was.

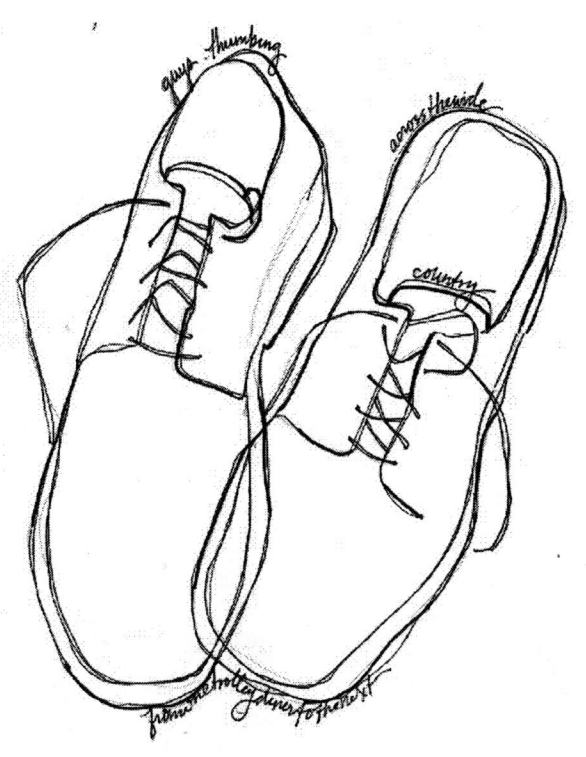

About the Author

Born in Brooklyn, New York, Marjorie Deiter Keyishian holds BA and MA degrees from Columbia University. Her poetry, fiction, and articles have appeared in a variety of journals, including *The Literary Review, The Massachusetts Review, The New York Times, Fiction, Ararat, New York Quarterly, The English Record, Northeast Journal, Inkwell, Graham House Review, Sparrow, Phoebe,* and *Outerbridge,* among others. She has served as editor of *The Journal of New Jersey Poets* and is at present contributing editor to *The Literary Review.* She teaches courses in poetry and contemporary fiction at Fairleigh Dickinson University in Madison, New Jersey.